The Kingdom Keys

"I will give you the keys to the kingdom of heaven. What you lock on earth will be locked in heaven. What you unlock on earth will be unlocked in heaven."

Matthew 16:19 (NIRV)

Tamara Brown

3G Publishing, Inc.
Loganville, Ga 30052
www.3gpublishinginc.com
Phone: 1-888-442-9637

©2016, Tamara Brown. All rights reserved.

No part of this book may be reproduced, stored in a retrieval system, or transmitted by any means without the written permission of the author.

First published by 3G Publishing, Inc., January, 2017.

ISBN: 9781941247334

Printed in the United States of America

Because of the dynamic nature of the Internet, any web addresses or links contained in this book may have changed since publication and may no longer be valid. The views expressed in this work are solely those of the author and do not necessarily reflect the views of the publisher, and the publisher hereby disclaims any responsibility for them.

DEDICATION

This book is dedicated to Jesus Christ, His kingdom, and those seeking a relationship with Him, to my husband and son, to the loving memory of my mother and grandmother. To my family and friends that supported, encouraged and prayed for me in the process of writing this book. I also dedicate this book to all of you, the readers; thank you for sowing into my vision.

Contents

DEDICATION — iii
PREFACE — ix
INTRODUCTION — xiii

The Seven Keys of Discipleship — 17

The Key of Worship — 19

Chapter One
  The First Key is to Understand
  Your Relationship with God — 21

The Key of Prayer — 25

Chapter Two
  The Second Key is To Turn to
  God in Prayer — 27

The Key of Praise — 37

Chapter Three
  The Third Key is to Praise Him — 39

The Key of God's Word — *41*

Chapter Four
  The Fourth Key is to utilize the Power of God's Word — 43

The Key of Ministry — *45*

Chapter Five
  The Fifth Key is Ministry through Discipleship — 47

The Key of Fellowship — *53*

Chapter Six
  The Sixth Key is Fellowship with One Another — 55

The Key of Testimony — *59*

Chapter Seven
  The Seventh Key is To Share Your Testimony — 61

How Keys Were Used in the Early Church — *63*

Chapter Eight
  Keys Essential to the Early Church — 65

Chapter Nine
  Revealing The Key of Knowledge   71

How Keys Apply To You
  The Keys to Success   73

Chapter Ten
  The Keys to Successful Living   75

It's Time for A Key Inventory!   77

Chapter Eleven
  Conducting a Key Inventory   79

Custodians of the Everlasting Keys   83

Chapter Twelve
  Custodians of the Everlasting Keys   85

Keys and the Last Day Church   89

Chapter Thirteen
  The Book of Revelation and
  the Key of Worship   91

PREFACE

Have you ever lost your keys? If so, you're familiar with the sense of frustration and inconvenience that the experience can bring. Keys are important because they give us access to certain places or things such as our homes, vehicles, offices and so forth. Although we may be the rightful owner or have authorized access, without keys we don't have what we need.

In a spiritual sense, each key unlocks or releases something that we need from God. The first key is worship. The Magi worshiped, the Demoniac worshiped, the Leper worshiped and the Disciples worshiped. Also, when the people of God were in distress they worshiped. What was the result? Deliverance was released to the Demoniac, healing was released to the Leper and victory was released to the people of God in battle. We worship God not based on what He can do for us, but for who He is. In His presence is fullness of joy and pleasures forevermore.

The second key is the key of prayer. God honors prayer and prayer honors God. Prayer is the opening of the heart to God as to a friend. Prayer is the key in the hand of faith that unlocks or releases heavenly resources. This key changes reality, for God changes things through prayer, and fasting intensifies prayer. When Peter was imprisoned, the church prayed and he was released by an angel. When Elijah prayed, a boy was released from the grip of death and his life was restored. When the thief on the cross prayed to Jesus he received salvation.

The third key is the key of praise, for God inhabits the praises of His people. This key invites God's presence and reveals the heart. Praise is the language of gratitude and comes forth from a heart filled with thanksgiving. Paul and Silas combined keys when they prayed and sang praises to God, which caused an earthquake and their release from prison chains. Paul and Silas didn't focus on their situation, but on God. Praise is the key to breakthrough and we should praise in the midst of adversity.

The fourth key is the Word of God. The Word is God's voice. This key dispels darkness and faith comes by hearing the Word. It is also used to resist temptation, prevent deception, sanctify and safeguard the heart. Jesus used this key against Satan in the wilderness to show the awesome power of God's word. Satan asked Jesus for worship; which is the first key.

The fifth key is the key of ministry. Ministry is meeting the needs of others in a godly way. Dorcas used this key to minister to the people and was resurrected for her ministry. This key relieves oppression, gives hope and is linked to the ministry of helps. The five-fold ministry of apostles, prophets, evangelists, pastors and teachers is designed for the work of the ministry. Therefore, whenever we have the opportunity, we should do good to everyone—especially to those in the family of faith.

The sixth key is the key of fellowship. If we walk in the light we have fellowship with one another; which leads to love relationships. When Paul and Silas were released from prison, they went to Lydia's house, a worshiper of God; where they met with brothers and sisters encouraging them. This key connects God's people, for a kingdom divided against itself cannot stand.

The seventh key is the key of testimony. This key puts God's power on display and bears witness to the truth. John the Revelator, bared record of the word of God, and of the testimony of Jesus Christ. Truly, we overcome by the blood of the Lamb and by the word of our testimony. God is faithful to His promise to give us the keys to the kingdom, but it's up to us to use them.

"I am he that liveth, and was dead; and, behold, I am alive for evermore, Amen; and have the keys of hell and of death." Revelation 1:18

INTRODUCTION

The Kingdom Keys is a book filled with inspirational information, revelation and the potential for transformation of its readers. It describes in detail, the seven keys of discipleship and how God's people have used them to maintain their connection with God. Most people use keys everyday of their lives and spiritual keys should be no different. Jesus wants to give you keys to the kingdom. Through prayer you can enter the kingdom by faith and confession unto salvation. (Romans 10:9-10)

Entering the Kingdom

If you declare with your mouth, "Jesus is Lord," and believe in your heart that God raised him from the dead, you will be saved. For it is with your heart that you believe and are justified, and it is with your mouth that you profess your faith and are saved. If you want life, hope and peace, let Jesus into your heart today. Invite Him to be your Savior and Lord to begin a loving relationship. No one can enter the kingdom unless born of water and of spirit. This is what it means by rebirth or being born again. As you draw near to Him with confession and repentance, He will draw near to you with mercy and forgiveness. (John 3:3-5)

Maintaining Kingdom Connection

Find a church where you can be baptized, learn about God's word, worship and fellowship with other Christians. Pray daily, never forget to be grateful to God and praise. Get involved in a ministry and share your testimony. These are the seven keys of discipleship. Whether you desire to enter the kingdom or are already in the kingdom, keys make life better and maintain a kingdom connection. (Hebrews 10:25)

In the Kingdom, divinity and humanity work together. God gave the blueprint, but Noah built the Ark. Moses held up his rod, then the Red Sea parted by the power of God. Israel marched around Jericho seven times, shouted with a mighty voice and then the walls of their enemies fell down.

The believer's ability to be fireproof; conquer a giant, survive the lion's den, survive the flood, interpret dreams, heal the sick, cause the lame to walk by faith, walk through the Red Sea, cast out spirits, possess incredible strength, receive supernatural wisdom, give Virgin birth, and resurrect the dead is due to relationship with God and the power of kingdom connection.
(John 15:5)

Faith Pleases God

One's connection is often preserved by refusal to compromise his or her faith. It was because of their refusal to worship an idol that caused the three Hebrew boys to be thrown into the fiery furnace. It was because of Daniel's refusal to stop his daily devotion to prayer that landed him in the lion's den. It was because of Paul and Silas' refusal to stop preaching the Gospel that caused them to be imprisoned.

Due to their refusal to give up in despair, they prayed and sang praises to God, resulting in deliverance. The keys of worship, prayer and praise was the ultimate test of their faith and loyalty to God. God doesn't give anything without purpose. Discover how kingdom keys have been used by people of faith throughout the centuries and how the keys to the kingdom can draw you deeper into God's presence. (Hebrews 11:6)

The Seven Keys of Discipleship

The Key of Worship

"Give unto the Lord the glory
due unto his name; worship
the Lord in the beauty of holiness."

Psalm 29:2

Chapter One

The First Key is to Understand Your Relationship with God through Worship

Abraham the Worshiper

This key requires humility. Worship is not merely a ritualistic practice, it is a lifestyle. One cannot truly worship God and remain prideful or unchanged. The first time the word worship is mentioned in scripture is in Genesis 22:5; which teaches the lesson of keeping God first. When we consider how much we sacrifice for God, it fails in comparison to how much He has sacrificed for us. Abraham was found to be a sacrificial worshiper because he truly loved God. His devotion to God went far beyond what he ever imagined. His worship experience found him to be faithful, forsaking all, even his beloved son Isaac. Abraham could have made excuses, because he waited so long to receive the fulfillment of God's promise or because he loved Isaac so much. Instead, Abraham grasped hold of the key of worship and obeyed God; demonstrating that obedience is better than sacrifice. When trial came to Abraham, God's friend, he was prepared to sacrifice his son. Abraham was a man of strong faith whom God made the Father of many nations. You are Abraham's seed, you're royalty, destined to reign and the kingdom of God is within you. As a worshiper, sacrifices must be made and tests and trials endured, but God is an ever present help in time of need.

> *"And Abraham said to his young men, "Stay here with the donkey; the lad and I will go yonder and worship, and we will come back to you."*
> **Genesis 22:5**

Job the Worshiper

Job was a righteous man that feared God and hated evil. When trial and tribulation came to Job, God's servant, he worshiped. Whether one is a friend of God, a servant or a son, the proper response to the love of God is worship. Job went through one of the most trying times that anyone has ever endured. He suffered loss of family, wealth and health, yet he did not curse God.

Job Restored

And the Lord turned the captivity of Job, when he prayed for his friends. He also gave Job twice as much as he had before. A worshiper isn't pressured to be in control. Although one's preparation may be adequate for the impact of the crisis, the timing and outcome must be released to God. Life experiences can be like that of Abraham or Job, causing separation, sacrifice or death, whatever the circumstance, we must worship in spirit and truth.

Job was steadfast, devoted and faithful, yet he was afflicted. Being a worshiper doesn't mean that life will be void of pain or suffering. Our lives are in constant conflict between worship and warfare. Job's calamity was not due to God, or his guilt, but Satan. The four key elements of worship are that it must be: exclusive, sincere, spiritual and truthful, for God seeks such worshipers. The opposite of worship is idolatry and anything or anyone put before God is false worship. To worship means loving God and people; it's yielding one's life and will to Him.

> *"Then Job arose, tore his robe, and shaved his head; and he fell to the ground and worshiped."*
> **Job 1:20**

Moses the Worshiper

Moses was a meek man and was a worshiper with an intimate relationship with the Lord. He was also a prayer intercessor for God's people. He had a vast range of experiences such as the Wilderness, Burning Bush, Red Sea and the Mountain Top experience. These life experiences shaped his character and prepared him for purpose. Through his connection with God, Moses' purpose was fulfilled as a faithful leader and deliverer of the Israelites. Through the Burning Bush experience, he received the call of God on his life and performed signs and wonders.

The Red Sea experience represents the supernatural power of God and His intervention on behalf of His people. The Wilderness experience, represents wandering, moving in circles, running from the past or rebellion. However, it also represents the process of learning valuable skills helpful in fulfilling one's God given purpose.

To be in the wilderness is being in the "interim place" between Egypt and the Promise Land, the destination. David was in an interim place for years; an anointed King, but not yet in the position. In the meantime, he was pursued by King Saul, running from place to place for his life. Are you in an interim place? There are things that you will learn about God and yourself in this season that reveals your character and identity as a worshiper of the living God.

The Mountain Top experience represents elevation, a time of intimacy, or receiving a greater revelation of who God is. Through each of these experiences, his relationship with God grew closer as he learned how to respond to God and react to mankind. God appeared before Moses at Mount Sinai, revealing His glory. He received the law of God; which is His express will and character.

"So Moses made haste and bowed his head toward the earth, and worshiped."
Exodus 34:8

The Key of Prayer

"If my people, who are called by my name, will humble themselves and pray and seek my face and turn from their wicked ways, then I will hear from heaven, and I will forgive their sin and will heal their land."

2 Chronicles 7:14

Chapter Two

The Second Key is To Turn to God in Prayer

This key requires faith. Prayer is maintaining communication with God. It is the privilege of every child of God to pray. Prayer honors God and God honors prayer. We can talk to humans that cannot change our situation one iota. We can rehearse life's difficulties, but it is only when we pray that we request Divine help. Rather than turning to God in prayer the Israelites murmured and complained in the wilderness. God responded by sending biting serpents that could not be charmed. As a result, they died by the thousands. The good news is that Moses gave Divine instruction to stay the plague and remedy their plight. King Hezekiah, upon receiving a death sentence from the Lord by the prophet Isaiah, turned to God in prayer, was healed and granted fifteen additional years of life. Prayer moves mountains. Do you have mountains in your life? Pray! If the saints of God with deep humility will fast and pray their prayers will prevail.

Jesus said, "Whatsoever ye ask in my name, that will I do, that the Father may be glorified in the Son."
John 14:13

Hannah the Prayer Warrior

Hannah turned to God in prayer and by faith touched God with her tears. He granted her request for a son; for she was barren and vowed to give her firstborn to Him. Her son Samuel grew up to be a Prophet; turning the hearts of an apostate people Godward. Hannah wanted a son, but God wanted a Prophet. Her prayer was radical, specific and in sync with God's will. If we ask God what He wants we sometimes get what we desire in the process. Like Hannah, we can go to the throne of grace for what we need and pray to the One who cares about the desires of our hearts. Hannah persevered in prayer and when her petition was granted she kept her vow to the Lord, leaving her son at the temple. And the child Samuel grew on, and was in favor with the Lord and also with men.

"So Hannah rose up after they had eaten in Shiloh, and after they had drunk. Now Eli the priest sat upon a seat by a post of the temple of the LORD. 10 And she was in bitterness of soul, and prayed unto the LORD, and wept sore. 11 And she vowed a vow, and said, "O LORD of hosts, if thou wilt indeed look on the affliction of thine handmaid, and remember me, and not forget thine handmaid, but wilt give unto thine handmaid a man child, then I will give him unto the LORD all the days of his life, and there shall no razor come upon his head. 12 And it came to pass, as she continued praying before the LORD, that Eli marked her mouth." 1 Samuel 1:9-12

"Hear my cry, O God; attend unto my prayer."
Psalm 61:1

Esther the Praying Queen

When the enemies of God's people plotted against them Esther called for a three day fast. She went before the king un-summoned under penalty of death. She did not shrink in fear, but courageously stepped up. She didn't get distracted by the power or wealth of the palace, but was faithful and focused. She represents those that God can use that are both faithful and focused. Her promotion from an orphan girl to queen was part of God's plan to deliver the Jews.

There is a great controversy between good and evil. God works through His people and Satan works through his. Prayer is necessary to bring forth the power of God in the earth. It is His will to work through our prayers not independent of them. When trouble comes your way, do you have a tendency toward fear and worry or prayer and fasting? Who knows whether you have come into the kingdom for such a time as this?

"Then Esther sent this reply to Mordecai: Go, gather together all the Jews who are in Susa, and fast for me. Do not eat or drink for three days, night or day. I and my attendants will fast as you do. When this is done, I will go to the king, even though it is against the law. And if I perish, I perish. So Mordecai went away and carried out all of Esther's instructions."
Esther 4:15-17

Joshua's Prayer

Joshua was Moses' faithful minister and successor, and when the time came he was prepared to step up and carry the torch as Israel's new leader. The Lord was with him and when he needed more time to fight the enemy, he turned to God in prayer. With God all things are possible. God will give you victory in battle, but you still must fight. Here, Joshua teaches us that God will even give us the ability to command nature, when we pray and believe. Like Jesus rebuked the boisterous winds and waves to be still, Joshua spoke to the sun and moon.

" Then spake Joshua to the LORD in the day when the LORD delivered up the Amorites before the children of Israel, and he said in the sight of Israel, Sun, stand thou still upon Gibeon; and thou, Moon, in the valley of Ajalon.

[13] And the sun stood still, and the moon stayed, until the people had avenged themselves upon their enemies. Is not this written in the book of Jasher? So the sun stood still in the midst of heaven, and hasted not to go down about a whole day."

Joshua 10:12-13

Prayer Releases God's Agenda

Prayer is the ultimate conversation, and Jesus taught the disciples to turn to God in prayer. He taught them to pray intentionally, continually, privately and without repetition. Jesus said, "So I tell you, whatever you ask for in prayer, believe that you have received it, and it will be yours." When God answers our prayers, it increases our faith and we trust and believe Him for more and more. Are you limiting the power of prayer in your life through unbelief?

Three Layers of Prayer

"Ask, and it shall be given you, seek, and ye shall find, knock and it shall be opened unto you:
For everyone that asketh receiveth, and he that seeketh findeth; and to him that knocketh it shall be opened."
Matthew 7:7-8

The Lord's Prayer

"After this manner therefore pray ye:
Our Father which art in heaven, Hallowed be thy name. Thy kingdom come, Thy will be done in earth, as it is in heaven. Give us this day our daily bread. And forgive us our debts as we forgive our debtors. And lead us not into temptation, but deliver us from evil; For thine is the kingdom, and the power and the glory, for ever. Amen"
Matthew 6:9-13

The Thief's Prayer Request

"And he said unto Jesus, Lord, remember me when thou comest into thy kingdom. And Jesus said unto him, Verily I say unto thee, Today shalt thou be with me in paradise."
Luke 23:42-43

The Prayer of Jabez

"And Jabez called on the God of Israel, saying, Oh that thou wouldest bless me indeed, and enlarge my coast, and that thine hand might be with me, and that thou wouldest keep me from evil, that it may not grieve me! And God granted him that which he requested."
1 Chronicles 4:10

King Solomon's Prayer

"Now when Solomon had made an end of praying, the fire came down from heaven, and consumed the burnt offering and the sacrifices; and the glory of the LORD filled the house."
2 Chronicles 7:1

"And the Lord appeared to Solomon by night, and said unto him, I have heard thy prayer, and have chosen this place to myself for a house of sacrifice."
2 Chronicles 7:12

"And it was so, that when Solomon had made an end of praying all this prayer and supplication unto the Lord, he arose from before the altar of the Lord, from kneeling on his knees with his hands spread up to heaven."
1 Kings 8:54

Jonah's Prayer

After receiving an assignment by God to go to Nineveh to warn the people of imminent danger of God's judgement, Jonah went toward Tarshish instead. For this act of willful disobedience, he was not punished, but he was swallowed up by a great fish, sparing his life. Beforehand, a sea storm arose and he instructed the men to throw him overboard, so that the sea would be calm. They reluctantly complied with Jonah's request. I imagine that the fish's belly was dark, wet and smelly for three days and Jonah must have been very hungry. Once delivered, he had a changed perspective and his stubbornness turned to willingness to obey. He arrived in Ninevah and the people repented of their sins for they hearkened to the voice of Jonah, God's servant. Sometimes disobedience gets us in situations that only the Almighty can undo, when we pray.

"Then Jonah prayed unto the LORD his God out of the fish's belly,

² And said, I cried by reason of mine affliction unto the LORD, and he heard me; out of the belly of hell cried I, and thou heardest my voice.

³ For thou hadst cast me into the deep, in the midst of the seas; and the floods compassed me about: all thy billows and thy waves passed over me.

⁴ Then I said, I am cast out of thy sight; yet I will look again toward thy holy temple.

⁵ The waters compassed me about, even to the soul: the depth closed me round about, the weeds were wrapped about my head.

⁶ I went down to the bottoms of the mountains; the earth with her bars was about me forever: yet hast thou brought up my life from corruption, O LORD my God

⁷ When my soul fainted within me I remembered the LORD: and my prayer came in unto thee, into thine holy temple.

⁸ They that observe lying vanities forsake their own mercy.

⁹ But I will sacrifice unto thee with the voice of thanksgiving; I will pay that that I have vowed. Salvation is of the LORD.

¹⁰ And the LORD spake unto the fish, and it vomited out Jonah upon the dry land."
Jonah 2:1-10

Daniel's Prayer Life

Daniel consistently prayed three times a day. He was resented by his enemies and due to the king's edict to bow to an idol, he was thrown into the lion's den. God who sits high and looks low delivered Daniel, but his enemies were destroyed. The prophet's enemies counted on Daniel's firm adherence to principle for the success of their plan. They weren't mistaken in their estimate of his character. He had incredible faith and refused to compromise. Daniel was a light in gross darkness as a shining star in the night.

"Now when Daniel knew that the writing was signed, he went into his house; and his windows being open in his chamber toward Jerusalem, he kneeled upon his knees three times a day, and prayed, and gave thanks before his God, as he did aforetime."
Daniel 6:10

Daniel's Deliverance

"My God hath sent his angel, and hath shut the lions' mouths, that they have not hurt me: forasmuch as before him innocency was found in me; and also before thee, O king, have I done no hurt. Then was the king exceedingly glad for him, and commanded that they should take Daniel up out of the den. So Daniel was taken up out of the den, and no manner of hurt was found upon him, because he believed in his God."
Daniel 6:22-23

Daniel the Prayer Intercessor

God seeks Intercessors, and Daniel lived to pray-on. Prayer is as vital to our spiritual well –being, as natural food is to our physical well-being. Prayer is the life-line of Christians and Satan trembles when God's people pray in faith. Why? God responds to faith. When the prayer of faith is combined with the shield of faith in the full armor of God, and the spiritual fruit of faith, we guard ourselves from the enemy of souls. Christians can find strength only at the throne of grace while humbly making known their wants and with strong cries and tears plead for heavenly strength to be fortified against the powerful temptations and snares of the Devil. Daniel saw his unworthiness before the Lord. Rather than claiming to be pure and holy, he humbly identified himself with the sinful of Israel. His godly wisdom was far superior to the wisdom of the world's great men. Yet consider the prayer from the lips of this man favored of Heaven. With deep humility, tears and rending of heart, he pleaded for himself and for his people. He opened his soul before God, confessing his own sins and acknowledging the Lord's greatness and majesty." The Sanctified Life, Chapter 53:7.

Daniel Prayed

"Oh Lord, the great and dreadful God, keeping the covenant and mercy to them that love him, and to them that keep his commandments; we have sinned, and have committed iniquity, and have done wickedly, and have rebelled, even by departing from thy precepts and from thy judgments; neither have we hearkened unto thy servants the prophets, which spoke in thy name to our kings, our princes, and our fathers, and to all the people of the land..."

Daniel 9:4-6

Touched By An Angel

"Yea, whiles I was speaking in prayer, even the man Gabriel, whom I had seen in the vision at the beginning, being caused to fly swiftly, touched me about the time of the evening oblation. And he informed me, and said O Daniel, I am now come forth to give thee skill and understanding."

Daniel 9: 21-22

The Key of Praise

"Give thanks to the LORD,
for his love endures forever."

2 Chronicles 20:21

Chapter Three

The Third Key is to Praise Him

David the Praising King

This key requires gratitude. The universal language of praise is Hallelujah! The garment of praise can be worn in every season of life. The worshiper worships God for who He is and the Praiser praises God for what He has done. In adversity and triumph, King David's life was marked by praise and worship. Once his praise was so radical that he danced with all his might before the Lord, but his wife didn't understand. David had a heart after God's own heart, he said, "I will bless the Lord at all times: his praise shall continually be in my mouth." What's in your mouth these days? Is it gossip, murmuring and complaining or is it praise? Enter into His gates with thanksgiving, and into His courts with praise. Have any of us considered how much we have to be thankful for? Do we remember that the mercies of the Lord are new every morning and that His faithfulness fails not? Do we acknowledge our dependence upon Him and express gratitude for His favor? To the contrary, we too often forget that "every good gift and every perfect gift is from above, and comes down from the Father of lights.

> *"O praise the LORD, all ye nations:*
> *praise him, all ye people."*
> **Psalm 117:1**

Praise Before Victory

Praise is a part of spiritual warfare. "When God's people went into battle against the enemy's army, praising the Lord with singing, and exalting the God of Israel. This was their battle song. They possessed the beauty of holiness. If more praising of God were engaged in now, hope and courage and faith would steadily increase. And would not this strengthen the hands of the valiant soldiers who today are standing in defense of truth? They praised God for the victory, and in the days thereafter the army returned to Jerusalem, laden with the spoils of their enemies, singing, praise for the victory won. Sons and Daughters of God, when we have a deeper appreciation of the mercy and loving kindness of God, we will praise Him, instead of complaining. We will talk of the loving watch care of the Lord, of the tender compassion of the Good Shepherd. The language of the heart will not be selfish murmuring. Praise, like a clear and flowing stream, will come from God's truly believing ones. Let us look back to where God has brought us from and exalt His name." Conflicts & Courage, page 218

> *"And when he had consulted with the people, he appointed singers unto the Lord, and that should praise the beauty of holiness, as they went out before the army, and to say, Praise the Lord; for his mercy endureth forever."*
> **2 Chronicles 20:21**

The Key of God's Word

"And take the helmet of salvation, and the sword of the Spirit, which is the word of God:"

Ephesians 6:17

Chapter Four

The Fourth Key is to utilize the Power of God's Word

Jesus the Living Word

This key requires the Holy Spirit. The Holy Spirit leads into all truth and gives one the ability to understand God's word; which is both powerful and life-changing. The scripture is the key that unlocks scripture and is the key to knowledge. Memorizing scripture helps to utilize power against the Enemy, especially in times of spiritual warfare. If there is no scripture memorized it is difficult, if not impossible to fight against the Adversary of souls.

"We receive Christ through His word, and the Holy Spirit is given to open the Word of God to our understanding and bring home its truths to our hearts." Lift Him Up, Page 131.

The keys of the kingdom of heaven are the words of Christ and they are spirit and life. The Kingdom of God is governed by the Word and is its authority. God's word is a lamp to the feet and light on the pathway. We need the light of God's word especially in times of darkness when there's limited visibility. When the word of God is planted in the heart it produces growth. However, when we neglect the word and prayer we do ourselves great disservice. (1 Peter 2:1-3)

Nothing can replace the holy, inerrant, infallible and inspired Word of God. The penetrating Word of God is multi-faceted; its seed to the sower, bread to the hungry, water to the thirsty, a map to the traveler, a love letter to the Church, a light in darkness and a sword to the soldier in battle. The Word of God is powerful, quick and sharper than a two-edged sword. Also, the word transforms and leads to consistency in the life. God's word rightly understood and applied is a safeguard and is part of the armor of God. "We can pray that as we read the Word, God will send His Spirit to reveal the truth that will strengthen our souls for today's need." Lift Him Up, Page 131.

"The grass withereth, the flower fadeth: but the word of our God shall stand for ever."
Isaiah 40:8

"In the beginning was the Word, and the Word was with God, and the Word was God."
John 1:1

"Sanctify them through thy truth: thy word is truth."
John 17:17

"Preach the word; be instant in season, out of season; reprove, rebuke, exhort with all long suffering and doctrine."
2 Timothy 4:2

The Key of Ministry

"For the perfecting of the saints, for the work of the ministry, for the edifying of the body of Christ."

Ephesians 4:12

Chapter Five

The Fifth Key is Ministry through Discipleship

Method of Christ

This key requires service to others. There are many who suffer in our world, look not every man on his own things, but every man also on the things of others. During his earthly ministry, Christ ministered to the masses and then bid them to, "Follow Me." The Lord needs laborers in His vineyard for the harvest is plentiful, but the workers are few. Some Christians become fat on the word, but lack ministry which is imbalanced. This can easily be remedied by praying to God about what capacity to serve. Being in the right lane of ministry maximizes our effectiveness in our service to others.

Ministry of Christ

Ministry is about allowing others to see Jesus in you. When the body of Christ uses their gifts and talents in service, the needs of the world will be met. Success depends not so much on talent as on energy and willingness. The gifts of the spirit are given for the perfecting of the saints, for the work of the ministry, for the edifying of the body of Christ: Till we all come in the unity of the faith, and of the knowledge of the Son of God, unto a perfect man, unto the measure of the stature of the fullness of Christ.

Maturity in Christ

May we mature in Christ, that we henceforth be no more children, tossed to and fro, and carried about with every wind of doctrine, by the sleight of men, and cunning craftiness, whereby they lie in wait to deceive; But speaking the truth in love may grow up into him in all things, which is the head, even Christ. Christ doesn't want his disciples to remain in spiritual infancy, but charges his disciples to reproduce by making disciples.

Peter the Anointed Minister

Jesus warned Peter that Satan desired to destroy Him. Satan wants the church to be unholy, unproductive, unfruitful, unfaithful, unloving, ungrateful, un-prayerful and altogether un-useful to God and mankind. Jesus used the key of prayer to strengthen Peter's faith.

"And the Lord said, Simon, Simon! Indeed, Satan has asked for you, that he may sift you as wheat. 32 But I have prayed for you, that your faith should not fail; and when you have returned to Me, strengthen your brethren."
Luke 22:31-32

The Ministry of Healing

After Peter's conversion, he became a powerhouse and an anointed minister for the Gospel. His lane of ministry was as healer and missionary. At the gate called Beautiful, it was Peter who addressed the lame man to take up his bed and walk; not John.

"Then Peter said, "Silver and gold I do not have, but what I do have I give you: In the name of Jesus Christ of Nazareth, rise up and walk." And he took him by the right hand and lifted him up, and immediately his feet and ankle bones received strength. So he, leaping up, stood and walked and entered the temple with them—walking, leaping, and praising God."
Acts 3:6-8

Peter Resurrects Dorcas with the Prayer Key

"Then Peter arose and went with them. When he was come, they brought him into the upper chamber: and all the widows stood by him weeping, and shewing the coats and garments which Dorcas made, while she was with them. 40 But Peter put them all forth, and kneeled down, and prayed; and turning him to the body said, Tabitha, arise. And she opened her eyes: and when she saw Peter, she sat up. 41 And he gave her his hand, and lifted her up, and when he had called the saints and widows, presented her alive."
Acts 9:39-41

Ministry Matters to God

The Kingdom of God has many wonderful ministries and one of my favorites is the ministry of music. Music is a universal language; it prepares the heart to receive deep spiritual truths and can have a calming effect upon the listener. Ministries such as the Couples Ministry, Discipleship Ministry, Health

Ministry, Homeless Ministry, Men's Ministry, Ministry of Helps, Nursing Home Ministry, Prayer Ministry, Prison Ministry, Singles Ministry, Women's Ministry, Youth Ministry and many others has impacted millions, both young and old.

Who has God placed in your path to minister to? He sent Peter to the house of Cornelius to share the gospel, and they were baptized; He sent Ananias to Saul to lay hands on him that he would regain sight and receive the Holy Spirit; He sent Elijah to a widow woman to sustain him and she received a miracle of oil and meal for many days. God can meet our needs without human help, but He chooses to use ordinary people to bless and minister to others.

"And the King shall answer and say unto them, Verily I say unto you, Inasmuch as ye have done it unto one of the least of these my brethren, ye have done it unto me."
Matthew 25:40

Angels in Our Midst

God created the Angels that minister to the heirs of salvation who in turn minister to others; which is continuity of God's grace. For centuries, Angels have been sent to deliver messages to mankind, to carryout God's judgement, to carry Lot and his family to safety, to give instructions to Samson's parents, to stop Abraham from slaying his son Isaac, to tell Mary about Jesus' birth, and to roll back the stone on Resurrection morning for the Savior . Hallelujah! Angels are often in our midst and some have entertained these heavenly beings unaware.

"Bless ye the Lord, all ye his hosts; ye ministers of his, that do his pleasure."
Psalm 103:21

Angels Minister to Christ

The Angels of the Lord ministered to Christ during his earthly ministry and after being tempted of Satan. Jesus continued preaching the gospel of the kingdom. God is fighting for us, pushing back the darkness, lighting up the kingdom that cannot be shaken, in the name of Jesus the enemy is a defeated foe. As we move about in the kingdom we have power to overcome because of the resurrection power that's alive within us.

"Then the devil leaveth him, and, behold, angels came and ministered unto him.
Matthew 4:11

"And he was there in the wilderness forty days, tempted of Satan; and was with the wild beasts; and the angels ministered unto him."
Mark 1:13

The Key of Fellowship

"But if we walk in the light, as he is in the light, we have fellowship with one another, and the blood of Jesus, his Son, purifies us from all sin."

1 John 1:7

Chapter Six

The Sixth Key is Fellowship with One Another

This key requires love and forgiveness. God is eternal, majestic, holy, powerful, loving, creative and relational. He who spoke the world into existence created us with fellowship in mind. He desires that we live the abundant life enjoying fellowship with one another; just as the Disciples had meaningful fellowship together. Fellowship gives us a sense of belonging and edifies one another. Family and friends is really God's way of loving us. Have you ever felt lonely and was called or visited? Didn't it make you feel better and uplifted your spirit? Connection with fellow believers not only enriches our lives, but when we need help during difficult times we are not alone. Furthermore, we have others with which to share life's joys.

Love is the master key. We need passion for Christ and compassion for people. We cannot love God without loving people. We cannot get to heaven alone, we need to master the art of relationship. In fact, relationships are meant to make us grow. The benefit of relationship or partnership is threefold: to exchange strengths, increase productivity and share in rewards.

There are four types of relationships within a lifespan. We are born into a family relationship and as we grow and develop, we enter into friendships. If we choose to marry, we enter a covenant relationship with a spouse. Finally, we enter relationship with Jesus Christ thereby joining the family of God. Enjoy your relationships as you walk in forgiveness and love.

Three of the most beautiful relationships in the Bible are between Naomi and Ruth, Jonathan and David, and Elijah and Elisha. Naomi and Ruth were mother in law and daughter in law. Jonathan and David were close friends, and Elijah and Elisha were mentor and protégé in ministry. Naomi, Jonathan and Elijah were coverings in their partnerships and their love relationships were demonstrative of God's love mandate to love one another.

Naomi & Ruth

"And she said, Behold, thy sister in law is gone back unto her people, and unto her gods: return thou after thy sister in law. 16 And Ruth said, Intreat me not to leave thee, or to return from following after thee: for whither thou goest, I will go; and where thou lodgest, I will lodge: thy people shall be my people, and thy God my God: 17 Where thou diest, will I die, and there will I be buried: the LORD do so to me, and more also, if ought but death part thee and me."
Ruth 1:15-17

Jonathan & David

"And it came to pass, when he had made an end of speaking unto Saul, that the soul of Jonathan was knit with the soul of David, and Jonathan loved him as his own soul. 2 And Saul took him that day, and would let him go no more home to his father's house. 3 Then Jonathan and David made a covenant, because he loved him as his own soul."

1 Samuel 18:1-3

Elijah & Elisha

"And it came to pass, when the LORD would take up Elijah into heaven by a whirlwind, that Elijah went with Elisha from Gilgal. 2 And Elijah said unto Elisha, "Tarry here, I pray thee; for the LORD hath sent me to Bethel. And Elisha said unto him, As the LORD liveth, and as thy soul liveth, I will not leave thee." So they went down to Bethel. 3 And the sons of the prophets that were at Bethel came forth to Elisha, and said unto him, Knowest thou that the LORD will take away thy master from thy head to day? And he said, Yea, I know it; hold ye your peace."

2 Kings 2:1-3

*"And it came to pass, when they were gone over, that Elijah said unto Elisha, Ask what I shall do for thee, before I be taken away from thee.
And Elisha said, I pray thee, let a double portion of thy spirit be upon me."*

2 Kings 2:9

The Key of Testimony

"And they overcame him by the blood of the Lamb, and by the word of their testimony; and they loved not their lives unto the death."

Revelation 12:11

Chapter Seven

The Seventh Key is to Share Your Testimony

This key requires sharing. Sharing one's testimony is a reminder of the goodness, love and faithfulness of God toward us. Use your testimony to draw others to Christ. Satan does not want the church to utilize its keys including sharing testimonies. Sharing one's testimony oftentimes encourages others who may have struggles to know that they too can overcome, if they put their trust in God. Sometimes a single phrase of testimony can set events in motion that affects someone else's life for eternity. The Christian life should be a living testimony. John the Baptist, Stephen and many of the disciples were martyred for their faith. They loved not their lives unto death and their tests become their testimony.

"Every day of our lives we need a manifestation of the converting power of God. There must be a continual yielding of self to do the will of God. Our will is not a sanctified will unless it is in harmony with His will. And if it is in harmony with His will, our actions will bear testimony to that fact. God will not leave us in darkness, not knowing whether we are serving Him or not. We have the Word, and our actions will bear testimony as to whether or not we are obeying that Word." Volume 2 Sermons and Talks, page 296.

A Living Testimony

At the onset of the Apostle Paul's conversion to Christianity, he received the Holy Spirit. He was a chosen vessel to preach the gospel to the Gentiles and suffer for Christ's name sake. By God's grace he transitioned from religion to relationship with Jesus Christ. Ironically, he had become that which he hated—a Christian. I am amazed at God's power to change our hearts in an instant. Paul's passionate hatred for Jesus and His followers became passionate love for Christ and His cause. He converted many to Christianity and wrote much of the New Testament.

Paul finished well, and at the end of his life he testified of his faithfulness toward God and God's faithfulness toward him. Rather than looking back with regret, he chose to look forward with the expectation of rewards. Do you have a tendency toward reflecting on regrets or focusing on future rewards? Paul said:

"For I am now ready to be offered, and the time of my departure is at hand. 7 I have fought a good fight, I have finished my course, I have kept the faith:

8 Henceforth there is laid up for me a crown of righteousness, which the Lord, the righteous judge, shall give me at that day: and not to me only, but unto all them also that love his appearing."
2 Timothy 4:6-8

How Keys Were Used in the Early Church

Kingdom Keys and the Early Church

"Then said Jesus to those Jews which believed on him, If ye continue in my word, then are ye my disciples indeed;"

John 8:31

Chapter Eight

Keys Essential to the Early Church

Through Christ, God gave the church a pathway to success and a winning edge. Four benefits of Christ's followers are: His presence, peace, promises and power. Jesus gives his disciples power over the enemy and protection. The early church was a powerful force for good. With God as their source, the disciples were key players in the plan of salvation. Christ was indeed their Pattern, as they went about preaching the gospel to a sinful, dying world. Their message of hope was received by many and rejected by a myriad of others. Today, we are the benefactors of the early church's sacrifices, resilience and their relentless faith.

> *"Bless the Lord, O my soul, and forget*
> *not all his benefits:"*
> **Psalm 103:2**

The success of the early church can be attributed to their unwavering faith and use of the Kingdom keys given by Christ. Imagine Jesus running up the mountain and hiding the keys to your purpose, calling and destiny in His garment. You will never reach your full potential unless you pursue Him. You must move, go higher and draw closer to Him. You must move from darkness to light, from fear to faith and sorrow to the joy of the Lord which is your strength. You would not give the keys to your home or vehicle to a stranger would you? You would give them to those that you know, love and trust. Believers have been loved with an everlasting love and entrusted with the keys to the kingdom, which gives us authority, access, rights, privileges and benefits that the world cannot obtain without a saving relationship with Christ.

"And they continued steadfastly in the apostles' doctrine and fellowship, and in breaking of bread, and in prayers. 43 And fear came upon every soul: and many wonders and signs were done by the apostles. 44 And all that believed were together, and had all things common; 45 And sold their possessions and goods, and parted them to all men, as every man had need. 46 And they, continuing daily with one accord in the temple, and breaking bread from house to house, did eat their meat with gladness and singleness of heart, 47 Praising God and having favor with all the people. And the Lord added to the church daily such as should be saved."
Acts 2:42-47

Jail House Praise

The keys of prayer, praise, and the Word were used when Paul and Silas were imprisoned for their witness, and casting out a familiar spirit from a girl. The end result of their key usage was the salvation of lost souls. The jailor and his family received Christ and baptism. God works through trouble to work His will in our lives. May we be released from the prison of complaining and find liberty in our praise. As long as we are in the will of God, good things are bound to happen. Satan's plans for the Apostle and his companion were thwarted by jail house praise. No matter where you are or what you're going through you still have a reason to praise.

"And at midnight Paul and Silas prayed, and sang praises unto God: and the prisoners heard them. 26 And suddenly there was a great earthquake, so that the foundations of the prison were shaken: and immediately all the doors were opened, and every one's bands were loosed. 27 And the keeper of the prison awaking out of his sleep, and seeing the prison doors open, he drew out his sword, and would have killed himself, supposing that the prisoners had been fled. 28 But Paul cried with a loud voice, saying, Do thyself no harm: for we are all here. 29 Then he called for a light, and sprang in, and came trembling, and fell down before Paul and Silas, 30 And brought them out, and said, Sirs, what must I do to be saved? 31 And they said, Believe on the Lord Jesus Christ, and thou shalt be saved, and thy house. 32 And they spake unto him the word of the Lord, and to all that were in his house."

Acts 16:25-32

The Disciples Worship Jesus

"22 And straightway Jesus constrained his disciples to get into a ship, and to go before him unto the other side, while he sent the multitudes away.

23 And when he had sent the multitudes away, he went up into a mountain apart to pray: and when the evening was come, he was there alone.

24 But the ship was now in the midst of the sea, tossed with waves: for the wind was contrary.

25 And in the fourth watch of the night Jesus went unto them, walking on the sea.

26 And when the disciples saw him walking on the sea, they were troubled, saying, It is a spirit; and they cried out for fear.

27 But straightway Jesus spake unto them, saying, Be of good cheer; it is I; be not afraid.

28 And Peter answered him and said, Lord, if it be thou, bid me come unto thee on the water.

29 And he said, Come. And when Peter was come down out of the ship, he walked on the water, to go to Jesus.

30 But when he saw the wind boisterous, he was afraid; and beginning to sink, he cried, saying, Lord, save me.

31 And immediately Jesus stretched forth his hand, and caught him, and said unto him, O thou of little faith, wherefore didst thou doubt?

32 And when they were come into the ship, the wind ceased.

33 Then they that were in the ship came and worshipped him, saying, Of a truth thou art the Son of God."
Matthew 14:22-33

He Is Risen

"1 In the end of the sabbath, as it began to dawn toward the first day of the week, came Mary Magdalene and the other Mary to see the sepulchre.

2 And, behold, there was a great earthquake: for the angel of the Lord descended from heaven, and came and rolled back the stone from the door, and sat upon it.

3 His countenance was like lightning, and his raiment white as snow:

4 And for fear of him the keepers did shake, and became as dead men.

5 And the angel answered and said unto the women, Fear not ye: for I know that ye seek Jesus, which was crucified.
6 He is not here: for he is risen, as he said. Come, see the place where the Lord lay.

⁷ And go quickly, and tell his disciples that he is risen from the dead; and, behold, he goeth before you into Galilee; there shall ye see him: lo, I have told you.

⁸ And they departed quickly from the sepulchre with fear and great joy; and did run to bring his disciples word.

⁹ And as they went to tell his disciples, behold, Jesus met them, saying, All hail. And they came and held him by the feet, and worshipped him."
Matthew 28:1-9

Chapter Nine

Revealing The Key of Knowledge

"Woe unto you, lawyers! for ye have taken away the key of knowledge: ye entered not in yourselves, and them that were entering in ye hindered."
Luke 11:52

It was to the shepherds of the field that the angels heralded Christ's birth. It was the wise men who traveled from a distant land, not the teachers of the law who had position, prestige and the admiration of men. The key of knowledge was in their hands to reveal and strengthen the inner man of the people. The seekers of the truth whose minds and hearts were open to the things of God, came in and went out of their presence empty.

A Warning to Religious Leaders

Their knowledge of God became pride and the temple a den of robbers. Perhaps they had become ritualistic losing their love for God. Simeon and Anna were chosen over the learned to be made aware of the Messiah's presence. This is a warning to all who keep the key of knowledge to themselves or hinder truth seekers.

The lawyers and leaders felt threatened by the Redeemer's authority and loved not His appearing. With the exception of the Apostle Paul, many of the religious sects were unable to transition from religion to relationship with the Law Giver. They were keepers of the law, but lost the spirit of the law which is love. To obey the law means loving God and loving man. The first four commandments pertain to our love for God and the other six pertain to our response to mankind. The law without love is legalism and the word law represents the acronym, Love Always Wins! (L.A.W.)

"The law of the Lord is perfect, converting the soul: the testimony of the Lord is sure, making wise the simple."
Psalm 19:7

Head Knowledge vs. Heart Knowledge

The chief priests and scribes sought how they might kill Jesus, joining the ranks of those with only head knowledge of God. Likewise, was Lucifer, Cain, Judas, the Rich Young Ruler, Ananias and his wife Sapphira. Among those with heart knowledge of God was Abraham, Job, Moses, Noah, Joseph and King David, who had a heart after God's own heart.

"My people are destroyed for lack of knowledge: because thou hast rejected knowledge, I will also reject thee, that thou shalt be no priest to me: seeing thou hast forgotten the law of thy God, I will also forget thy children."
Hosea 4:6

"The fear of the Lord is the beginning of knowledge: but fools despise wisdom and instruction."
Proverbs 1:7

How Keys Apply To You

The Keys to Success

"This Book of the Law shall not depart from your mouth, but you shall meditate in it day and night, that you may observe to do according to all that is written in it. For then you will make your way prosperous, and then you will have good success."

Joshua 1:8

Chapter Ten

The Keys to Successful Living

Refusing Discouragement

Do you associate prayer with success? Along the journey to heaven there may be times when you feel like giving up. Perhaps you've prayed and fasted, believed, made positive confessions and stood on the word of God. Yet you cannot see the hand of God nor hear the voice of God. Be encouraged, using keys isn't magical, their use is subject to the timing and will of God and the key to success is refusing to be discouraged.

Rejecting Sin

For instance, David prayed and fasted but nevertheless, his first born child with Bathsheba died. David didn't get discouraged or angry with God, he worshipped. By God's grace they were given another child, Solomon who grew up to be king and built the temple of the Lord. He used the key of prayer to govern God's people and was the wisest man to ever live. However, it is important for us to note that our prayers can be hindered by sin.

Rejoicing in Hope

Where there's a key, there is yet hope. Even when we experience delay, it does not mean denial. Along our journey to heaven are many lessons, tests and trials, but we must trust the Almighty through it all. Don't worry about tomorrow because God is already there. He is in control of our past, present and future. If it seems the keys aren't working, wait on the Lord and be of good courage, wait I say on the Lord. Jesus gives us hope by giving us Himself.

"Rejoice in the Lord always: and again I say, Rejoice."
Philippians 4:4

Relying on God

God has given us his love, Son, Spirit, Word, Angels, Prophets, Promises and Keys; all is needed for a successful and prosperous life. We can put confidence in God's provision and rely upon Him. Although self-sufficiency is acclaimed in the world, reliance on God produces abundant living in His Kingdom. Thank Him for the difficulties in life, since they provide protection from the idolatry of self-reliance.

Remembering God's Word

We can experience God's best for us when we refuse to be discouraged, reject sin, rejoice, rely on God and remember His word. We cannot be successful without prayer and meditating on God's word followed by life application. Prosperity and success come from obedience to the word of the Lord. Worldly success is obtained by any means necessary, but true success honors God.

It's Time for A Key Inventory!

"Examine yourselves to see whether you are in the faith; test yourselves. Do you not realize that Christ Jesus is in you—unless, of course, you fail the test?"

2 Corinthians 13:5

Chapter Eleven

Conducting a Key Inventory

They keys of the kingdom are significant because they help us to live victorious lives. Using the seven keys is a vital part of discipleship because their use is a consistent reminder of God. Periodic key inventory should be conducted using the Word of God because our lives must be lived according to the Word. Key inventory makes us aware when something is missing from our Christian walk. Whenever I feel disconnected from God I conduct a key inventory, not as a checklist that I check off for good behavior, but rather as a check and balance.

Self-examination with questions such as, "Am I walking in the flesh or in the spirit? Am I utilizing the resources available to me as a child of the King? Am I worshipping God in my lifestyle? Am I spending time in prayer and interceding in prayer for others? Do I have an attitude of gratitude and praise? Am I studying God's word and applying it to my life? Am I serving others? Am I gathering people to Christ or scattering them? Do I demonstrate love? Am I quick to forgive or do I hold grudges? Am I sharing my faith or testimony when prompted by the Holy Spirit to do so?" Am I disciplined? Am I growing in my faith?

Self-examination reveals one's true character, motives and attitudes by reflecting inwardly. This will position you to receive your blessing from God, but most of all you truly become a vessel God can use to advance His kingdom. You've been chosen to do a work that only God can empower you to do. Therefore, it helps you to detect if you have wandered away from the Father's presence. Don't be afraid to know where you are because God is waiting for you to turn back to Him to fulfill your purpose.

Lost Keys

Has the church lost her keys? Zion is the church of Christ, it is global and diverse. Zion must return to her first love and utilize every key to her advantage. She too must overcome; for Christ has overcome the world before her. In the United States, prayer has been removed from public schools and people are sometimes forbidden to pray in the name of Jesus in open forums, such as sports events, political circles and in the military. The Ten Commandments have been removed from state property including court houses. Without the key of prayer, we tread upon dangerous ground. Without the key of God's word, we stumble in darkness, until we embrace gross darkness and reject the light. For self-examination purposes, conduct a key inventory in light of God's word:

Worship Key

[23]But the hour cometh, and now is when the true worshippers shall worship the Father in spirit and in truth: for the Father seeketh such to worship him.

[24]God is a Spirit: and they that worship him must worship him in spirit and in truth.
John 4:23-24

Prayer Key

Pray without ceasing.
1 Thessalonians 5:17

Praise Key

Praise ye the Lord. Praise God in his sanctuary: praise him in the firmament of his power. Praise him for his mighty acts: praise him according to his excellent greatness. Praise him with the sound of the trumpet: praise him with the psaltery and harp. ...
Psalm 150

Word Key

Study to shew thyself approved unto God, a workman that needeth not to be ashamed, rightly dividing the word of truth.
2 Timothy 2:15

Ministry Key

Learn to do well; seek judgment, relieve the oppressed, judge the fatherless, plead for the widow.
Isaiah 1:17

Fellowship Key

If we say that we have fellowship with him, and walk in darkness, we lie, and do not the truth:

"But if we walk in the light, as he is in the light, we have fellowship one with another, and the blood of Jesus Christ his Son cleanseth us from all sin.
1 John 1:6-7

Testimony Key

"And he commanded us to preach unto the people, and to testify that it is he which was ordained of God to be the Judge of quick and dead."
Acts 10:42

May God unleash your full potential in Christ. The keys to the kingdom promised by Jesus are part of your identity or essence. For example, there's the key of worship and you are a worshiper, the key of prayer and you are a prayer warrior, the key of praise and you are a praiser, the key of ministry and you are a minister.

Custodians of the Everlasting Keys

"I will place on his shoulder the key to the house of David; what he opens no one can shut, and what he shuts no one can open."

Isaiah 22:22

Chapter Twelve

Custodians of the Everlasting Keys

Elijah Uses the Key of Prayer

"Hear me, O LORD, hear me, that this people may know that thou art the LORD God, and that thou hast turned their heart back again. 38 Then the fire of the LORD fell, and consumed the burnt sacrifice, and the wood, and the stones, and the dust, and licked up the water that was in the trench. 39 And when all the people saw it, they fell on their faces: and they said, The LORD, he is the God; the LORD, he is the God."

1 Kings 18:37-39

The key custodian role is responsible for key management. Elijah, God's messenger was so connected to the God of heaven that heaven backed him up. Elijah had the everlasting keys and was taken up to heaven by whirlwind in a chariot of fire, without tasting death. He had been God's instrument for the overthrow of gigantic evils.

Elijah had victory after victory in his life. He was anointed and on the move for God. Moving by the power of God, he was a man of incredible faith, earnest prayer and deep moral conviction. He was instrumental in the showdown between the priests of Baal and the God of Israel. Christians are like modern day Elijah's and custodians of the keys. The prayer of faith is the great strength of the Christian and will surely prevail against Satan.

It is the responsibility of Christians to utilize every key to their advantage, for they help to navigate through life challenges. Today, weekly worship services should include all seven of the spiritual keys including worship, prayer, praise, the Word of God, ministry, Christian fellowship and testimonials.

Elisha Uses the Key of Prayer

"And he answered, Fear not: for they that be with us are more than they that be with them. 17 And Elisha prayed, and said, LORD, I pray thee, open his eyes, that he may see. And the LORD opened the eyes of the young man; and he saw: and, behold, the mountain was full of horses and chariots of fire round about Elisha. 18 And when they came down to him, Elisha prayed unto the LORD, and said, Smite this people,

I pray thee, with blindness. And he smote them with blindness according to the word of Elisha."
2 Kings 6:16-18

Jairus Uses the Key of Worship

The Divinity of Christ was worshiped by those who recognized the Majesty of Heaven. Those who worship Him find the exalted place at His feet. Some will remain trapped in their condition unless a key is used on their behalf. The ruler's daughter and the Syrophenician woman's daughter were healed because their parents had faith in the Son of God, the Great Physician.

"While he spake these things unto them, behold, there came a certain ruler, and worshipped him, saying, My daughter is even now dead: but come and lay thy hand upon her, and she shall live.

¹⁹ And Jesus arose, and followed him, and so did his disciples.

²³ And when Jesus came into the ruler's house, and saw the minstrels and the people making a noise,

²⁴ He said unto them, Give place: for the maid is not dead, but sleepeth. And they laughed him to scorn.

²⁵ But when the people were put forth, he went in, and took her by the hand, and the maid arose."
Matthew 9:18,19,23,24,25

The Syrophenician Woman Uses the Worship Key

*^{25} "For a certain woman, whose young daughter
had an unclean spirit, heard of him,
and came and fell at his feet:*

*^{26} The woman was a Greek, a Syrophenician by
nation; and she besought him that he would cast
forth the devil out of her daughter.*

*^{27} But Jesus said unto her, Let the children first
be filled: for it is not meet to take the children's
bread, and to cast it unto the dogs.*

*^{28} And she answered and said unto him, Yes, Lord:
yet the dogs under the table
eat of the children's crumbs.*

*^{29} And he said unto her, For this saying go thy way;
the devil is gone out of thy daughter.*

*^{30} And when she was come to her house, she found
the devil gone out, and her daughter
laid upon the bed."*
Mark 7:25-30

Keys and the Last Day Church

Fear not, little flock; for it is your Father's good pleasure to give you the kingdom.

Luke 12:32

Chapter Thirteen

The Book of Revelation and the Key of Worship

Have you ever stopped to think about God as Creator? God's love is as vast and wide as an ocean without bottom or shore. He loves unconditionally those for whom Christ died. The heavenly messenger proclaims to the earth's inhabitants to reverence, glorify and worship the Creator, whom made everything for His good pleasure and humanity's benefit.

We are living in a world filled with people that do not fear, glorify nor worship God. Worship is a sign of loyalty to the Great I AM. Worship is the seal of God and the Holy Spirit is the great Sealer. We were born with a desire to worship and if we don't worship God, we will worship someone, something or self. God deserves our worship, but Satan desires our worship. A final test for earth's inhabitants will be concerning worship. Lucifer, Satan, the Dragon, also called the Old Serpent lifted up his heart in pride rather than humility and worship of the Almighty.

"How art thou fallen from heaven, O Lucifer, son of the morning! How art thou cut down to the ground, which didst weaken the nations!

[13] For thou hast said in thine heart, I will ascend into heaven, I will exalt my throne above the stars of God: I will sit also upon the mount of the congregation, in the sides of the north: 14 I will ascend above the heights of the clouds; I will be like the most High. 15 Yet thou shalt be brought down to hell, to the sides of the pit."
Isaiah 14:12-15

Worship, a Test of Loyalty

"He that leadeth into captivity shall go into captivity: he that killeth with the sword must be killed with the sword. Here is the patience and the faith of the saints. 11 And I beheld another beast coming up out of the earth; and he had two horns like a lamb, and he spake as a dragon. 12 And he exerciseth all the power of the first beast before him, and causeth the earth and them which dwell therein to worship the first beast, whose deadly wound was healed."
Revelation 13:10-12

"And I saw another angel fly in the midst of heaven, having the everlasting gospel to preach unto them that dwell on the earth, and to every nation, and kindred, and tongue, and people, 7 Saying with a loud voice, Fear God, and give glory to him; for the hour of his judgment is come: and worship him that made heaven, and earth, and the sea, and the fountains of waters."
Revelation 14:6-7

"And the smoke of their torment ascendeth up for ever and ever: and they have no rest day nor night, who worship the beast and his image, and whosoever

receiveth the mark of his name. 12 Here is the patience of the saints: here are they that keep the commandments of God, and the faith of Jesus."
Revelation 14:11-12

Worship in the New Heaven and Earth

*"For as the new heavens and the new earth, which I will make, shall remain before me, saith the LORD, so shall your seed and your name remain.
23 And it shall come to pass, that from one new moon to another, and from one sabbath to another, shall all flesh come to worship before me, saith the LORD."*
Isaiah 66:22-23

King Jesus

*²² Look unto me, and be ye saved, all the ends of the earth: for I am God, and there is none else.
²³ I have sworn by myself, the word is gone out of my mouth in righteousness, and shall not return, That unto me every knee shall bow,
every tongue shall swear."*
Isaiah 45:22-23 NKJV

Jesus is the way, the truth and the life and He is the door to our destiny. Jesus said, "I am the door: by me if any man enter in, he shall be saved, and shall go in and out, and find pasture." John 10:9

The book of Revelation is the word of Jesus Christ speaking to His people, to show His servants things that must shortly come to pass. He sent and signified it by His angel to His servant John. Blessed are those who read it and hear the words of prophecy and keep those things written therein for the time is at hand.

A Final Word

God designed worship for us to see Him in His glory and to respond appropriately. Worship is the proper response to God's love, praise is the proper response to God's goodness and obedience is the proper response to God's Word. As we draw near to God in submission and resist the Devil he will flee. When Satan asked Jesus for the worship key, he received the word key instead.

> ***"And Jesus answered him saying, "It is written that Man shall not live by bread alone, but by every word of God."***
> ## Luke 4:4

Satan in these last days desires to receive our worship and we must respond like Jesus. May God give us a heart of worship, as we experience His presence, His love and His power.

> ***"Wherefore we receiving a kingdom which cannot be moved, let us have grace, whereby we may serve God acceptably with reverence and godly fear:"***
> ## Hebrews 12:28

www.ingramcontent.com/pod-product-compliance
Lightning Source LLC
Chambersburg PA
CBHW070654050426
42451CB00008B/340